Dancing in the Sky

Song by Dani and Lizzy Nelson

Tell me, what does it look like in heaven?
Is it peaceful? Is it free like they say?
 Does the sun shine bright forever?
Have your fears and your pain gone away?

'Cause here on Earth, it feels like everything Good is missing since
you left And here on Earth, everything's different There's an
emptiness

Oh-oh, I
hope you're dancing in the sky
 hope you're singing in the angel's choir
And I hope the angels know what they have
I'll bet it's so nice up in Heaven since you arrived

So tell me, what do you do up in Heaven?
Are your days filled with love and light?
Is there music? Is there art and adventure?
Tell me, are you happy? Are you more alive?

'Cause here on Earth, it feels like everything
Good is missing since you left
And here on Earth, everything's different There's an emptiness

oh-oh, I
I hope you're dancing in the sky
And I hope you're singing in the angel's choir
And I hope the angels know what they have
I'll bet it's so nice up in Heaven since you arrived

I hope you're dancing in the sky
And I hope you're singing in the angel's choir
And I hope the angels know what they have
I'll bet it's so nice up in Heaven since you arrived
since you arrived

I'M DANCING IN THE SKY

BY :

ROBIN LYNN MITCHELL - TAFOYA

COPYRIGHT

I'M DANCING IN THE SKY

Copyright © 2026 by ROBIN LYNN MITCHELL - TAFOYA

All rights reserved.

DEDICATION

To everyone who has lost a loved one. I am here to help and give a little love and compassion. My story is only for some direction.
(Something that I didn't have at all)
Also a Huge **THANK YOU to BOOK PLANETS** for helping me put my story and emotions together.
THANK YOU LOSLUNAS NM LIBRARY for helping me on the computer and printing out my manuscript for my book over and over to proofread.
And to all that stood by myside ♡

QUOTE:
"If everybody got somebody by the Hand Maybe everyone could learn and understand" – Sebastian Little Mermaid

ABOUT THE AUTHOR

My name is Robin Lynn Mitchell-Tafoya. I am 64 years old. This is my First Book. There will be 3 more books following this one in 2026. (Second Book Children's book Third Book Death in the hospital and Fourth Book is on about being scam). My son Bo was born with Down Syndrome and on the Autistic Spectrum. We are from New Mexico born and raised. On the most part he was high function. He loved life and everyday enjoyed learning and helping out.

QUOTE:

"You're braver than you believe and stronger than you seem, and smarter than you think"......!!! – Christopher Robin of winning the Pooh.

TABLE OF CONTENTS

CHAPTER 1
THE BOY WHO LOVED THE SKY

There are children who walk into the world quietly, and there are children who seem to arrive carrying a glow that everyone around them can feel before they even understand it. My son Bo belonged to the second group. From the moment I held him, I sensed that his life would be different, not because of his disability, but because of the tenderness he carried inside him. His eyes were the first thing people noticed. They were bright blue, like the early morning sky before the day warms up, and they sparkled every time he smiled. Those eyes watched everything with curiosity and love. They were the truest windows into the softness of his spirit.

Bo loved anything that lived and breathed. He was raised in the country, surrounded by animals that became part of his daily world. He fed miniature horses, brushed full-sized ones, helped gather eggs from the ducks, (he chased them and giggled so hard), he tossed feed to his cow, he even shared his bottle when he was smaller with the cow (MooMoo) and ran around the yard with our dogs trailing after him. Anyone who saw him outside would think he had been born to live among those animals. They followed him as if he carried a magnet inside his chest. Even the most skittish creatures settled when he came near. He moved slowly, gently, and always with patience. If a horse stamped its hoof or a cow shied away, he would stand still until they felt safe again. That was the way he loved, without rush and without demand. Animals seem to understand that kind of soul almost immediately.

The country air shaped him. He woke up with the sun and pressed his face against the window to look at the sky before he even stretched his arms. The sky mattered to him in a way I did not understand at first. He looked at clouds as if they were people he recognized. When a bird flew across the yard he whispered his thoughts to it. He was not loud by nature. Most of the time he would hum or talk to himself while he helped me outside. His voice had a rhythm that made ordinary chores feel like a small ceremony. He made feeding the dogs feel special. He made sweeping the porch feel peaceful. Everything became gentler when he was near it.

Because we lived in the country, the world was still and quiet most days. The roads were unpaved, the fields wide, and the sound of animals drifting in the distance was a normal part of life. Bo grew up in this calm place with an innocence that made people love him instantly. Strangers did not frighten him. He waved at everyone he saw and smiled at them as if he had known them for years. If someone stopped to talk to him, he always listened with the full weight of his attention. He wanted people to feel seen, even if he did not understand every word they said. People often walked away with tears in their eyes because something about him softened them. He had a way of reminding people that kindness could be simple.

There were many things Bo enjoyed, but nothing fascinated him like movies. He collected them the way other children collect toys. Every time a new film came out, he asked for it. He did not care about the price or whether the story matched his age. He just wanted to watch the characters move across the screen in colors and sounds that pulled him into their world. Movies became his language. They helped him understand emotions that were difficult to explain in ordinary conversation.

Two of his favorites stayed with him throughout his life. One was The Lion King. The other was All Dogs Go to Heaven. He memorized entire scenes from both films. He repeated dialogue in his own special voice. When Mufasa died in The Lion King, Bo asked questions only a child with a pure heart could ask. He wondered where Mufasa went. He wondered why Simba cried. He wondered how someone could disappear but still be loved. Those were questions I knew I would eventually have to answer in real life, but I put them away at the time. I thought we had years before he needed to understand the meaning of loss.

The second movie held a different kind of power. All Dogs Go to Heaven made him laugh and made him think. He loved Charlie and Itchy. He loved the idea that animals could live again in a place above the sky. He repeated the lines from that film with excitement, especially the scene where Charlie is warned that he cannot return once he leaves heaven. Bo liked to imitate the tone of the voice in that moment. He would open his eyes wide, start the sentence with a high pitch, and let his voice fall off into a soft whisper by the time he reached the last word. It was his way of acting, and I always laughed because he did it with such dramatic seriousness.

Movies did not just entertain him. They became teaching tools for me. When Bo was confused or worried, I used his favorite scenes to explain things. Stories helped him make sense of life, and I learned to speak through the characters he loved. If something frightening happened, I used a movie moment to guide him through his fear. If something joyful happened, I used another scene to celebrate with him. These films became bridges between his mind and the world around him.

Bo's disability shaped how he understood things, but it never limited his ability to feel deeply. Children with Down syndrome often carry an emotional intuition that surprises even the adults who care for them. They love without hesitation. They comfort without being asked. Bo was like that. If someone in the house was upset, he felt it immediately. He looked at faces closely and could tell when someone was sad or tired. His hands were small but warm, and he used them to wipe tears from cheeks as if he held the responsibility of healing in his fingertips. I often wondered how someone so young could carry so much gentleness inside him.

The people he loved the most were his grandfather, whom he called Papa, and my mother, whom he called Him. Those names were his own creation. He had his own language and his own way of identifying the people closest to him. Papa and Him were not just family. They were anchors in his world. He followed his grandfather outside, watched him work, and helped him whenever he could. When my stepfather needed oxygen or medication, Bo was right there handing him what he needed. Caring for someone gave him pride. Helping made him feel like he was part of something important.

Papa taught him how to fish. Also my mother was always planting flowers and Bo loved to help. He always bought her flowers. He loved to sit with my mother and listen to her talk. She would tell him stories about her childhood or talk about her day, and he would nod as if every word held secret meaning. He looked at her with a kind of awe that only children can show. He loved her so much that he used to hold her face with both hands when he wanted to say something meaningful. She always laughed because he did it with such intensity. I

4

do not think he ever realized how special that gesture was, but she treasured it.

Our life moved peacefully for many years. We did simple things together. We cooked meals. We prayed before dinner. We sat outside and listened to the sounds of the country. Bo had routines that shaped his evenings. Bubble baths. Snacks. A movie before bed. Prayers with interlocked fingers. His version of amen was always the same. He pulled his hands apart, lifted them into the air, and said goodbye to the ceiling with a smile. He did this every night, and every time he did it, he looked as though he was sending a message to someone above us.

I did not realize then how important these routines would become. I did not know how much strength they would give me later. At the time, they were just moments in our day. They were habits that made Bo feel safe and loved. They were the normal rhythms of a simple country life.

Still, even in those early days, I felt a strange whisper inside me. I did not know what it meant, but there were moments when I looked at my son and felt a quiet urgency. It was not fear. It was something else. As if I needed to prepare him for a world that would not always be gentle. As if I knew that the lessons I taught him would someday matter more than I expected. I did not talk about this feeling to anyone. I kept it tucked away, unsure of what it meant, hoping it was only my imagination.

But the truth is that children like Bo force you to see the world differently. They remind you that life is fragile and precious. They also remind you that love can change shape. It can settle into routines, expand into laughter, or hold steady in silence. It can make a small house feel full even when nothing extraordinary is happening.

Bo gave every day its own heartbeat. He made the house feel alive. When he laughed, the walls seemed brighter. When he played with the dogs outside, the whole yard felt lighter. When he sat with me and watched the clouds, I felt closer to something sacred. He made ordinary life feel holy. Not because of grand moments or dramatic events, but because of the way he loved. It was uncomplicated. It was pure. It was complete.

At that time, I had no idea that his fascination with the sky would become a symbol I clung to later. I had no idea that the movies he loved would become tools for survival. I had no idea that his innocence would become my guide through grief. All I knew was that my son loved the sky. He loved animals. He loved people. He loved stories. And I loved him more than I ever thought a heart could hold.

This chapter of our life was the calm before a storm I never saw coming. It was the season of sunshine, laughter, and the gentle simplicity of raising a boy whose heart was brighter than anything around him. If I had known what the future held, I would have held on to these days even tighter. But I am grateful for every moment we shared, because they shaped the foundation of everything that came later. They taught me how to see the world the way he saw it. Through awe. Through innocence. Through love.

And through the sky he loved so much.

ACTIVITIES

Part 1: My Garden of Love

Bo felt a deep connection to the animals, the broad sky, and his loving family. We all have a "Garden of Love" inside us—a special place where we keep the things that make our hearts feel full.

Take a moment to imagine your own garden. Think about:

- The people who love you.
- The pets who make you smile.
- The things in nature, like the sun or the trees, that make you feel peaceful.

Creative Idea: On a separate sheet of paper, you can draw your own garden and fill it with these special people and things. You can keep your drawing in a journal or put it on your wall to remind you of your connections.

CHAPTER 2
WHEN PAPA GOT HIS WINGS

There are moments in life that split time into a before and an after. For our family, the beginning of that divide arrived slowly, the way dusk fades into night. My stepfather, whom Bo adored and called Papa, had always been a steady presence in our home. He was not loud or demanding. He carried himself with quiet strength, the kind that does not need to announce itself. He taught Bo how to feed the animals and how to hold a bucket without spilling grain. He taught him how to pat a horse gently on the neck and how to walk around a cow with caution. Papa became one of the safest people in Bo's world. Because of that, Bo's heart wrapped itself tightly around him.

As time passed, Papa's health began to falter. It did not happen in a sudden way. At first it was small things that most people would shrug off. A little fatigue. A little heavy breathing. A few moments each day where he needed to sit before standing again. None of us noticed a drastic shift at first because Papa never wanted to worry anyone. He moved slower, but he still moved with the same stubborn pride. Even when the doctor placed him on oxygen, he shrugged it off in front of Bo, unwilling to frighten him. Bo helped him carry the tubing, hold the tank steady, and fetch his medications with the concentration of someone performing an important job. Helping Papa gave him purpose.

The house took on a different rhythm during those months. Machines made soft noises in the background. Oxygen hissed in quiet pulses. Medications lined the counter like soldiers waiting for instruction. Through it all, Bo watched every detail. He sensed change long before he understood it. When someone he loved did not feel well, his whole body responded. He hovered near Papa, placing a hand on his knee, leaning close to make sure he was still breathing easily.

Children like Bo carry a tenderness that borders on sacred, and he poured that tenderness into every moment he shared with Papa.

The day Papa's health took a serious turn began like any other. We were all in the house together. Bo was watching television and humming softly, and I was moving between the kitchen and the living room. My mother stayed close to her husband, keeping an eye on him with the anxious love that grows between people who have shared a lifetime. His breathing worsened that afternoon, and suddenly the effort seemed too great for him. I knew that we had reached a point where home care could no longer hold him safely. When the short breaths became strained ones, I called for help.

The sound of an ambulance siren is something most people hear from a distance. It is an echo that passes by and fades. When it stops in front of your home, it takes on a different meaning. The flashing lights wash across your yard. The air thickens with urgency. Every sense sharpens. For Bo, the arrival of an ambulance meant only one thing. In his understanding, an ambulance symbolized an owie. That was the word I had always taught him. Whenever we saw one passing on the road, I told him that someone had an owie and the ambulance was helping them. It was the simplest way to help him make sense of something frightening.

When the paramedics walked through our door, Bo froze. He did not cry or yell. He simply stared at them with wide blue eyes, trying to understand why they were in his safe place. He followed them as they moved toward Papa. When they lifted Papa onto the stretcher, the realization began to take shape inside him. He looked at Papa, then at me, and then back at Papa again with confusion tightening his expression. He could not understand why Papa was leaving him.

My mother stood beside me, her face pale with fear and grief. She clutched her hands together as the paramedics prepared to roll Papa outside. I could feel my heart pounding, not because of the emergency itself, but because I knew the weight of what Bo was seeing. For a child with Down syndrome, change can be jarring. For Bo, who loved with such depth, this moment felt like the ground shifting beneath us.

The paramedics noticed his distress and did something I will always be grateful for. They invited Bo into the back of the ambulance before they closed the doors. They let him lean over Papa, hold his hand, and kiss his cheek. Bo touched Papa's face gently and whispered something the rest of us could not hear. Then he placed his forehead against Papa's hand and stayed there for a moment. When Bo lifted his head, his eyes filled with worry. He looked at me for reassurance, searching for words that could explain a situation too large for him to grasp. All I could tell him was that Papa was sick and the doctors needed to help him.

That moment was the last time he ever saw Papa alive.

After the ambulance left, a stillness settled over the house. Bo walked from room to room calling out Papa's name. He opened the bathroom door. He looked under blankets. He checked behind doors as if Papa was playing a game of hide and seek. Each time he did not find him, his confusion deepened. My mother began to cry at the kitchen table, her face buried in her hands. I stood beside her, trying to think of how to make this easier for Bo. Nothing felt adequate.

Papa was taken to the hospital, and when his condition did not improve, he was moved to a nursing home for hospice care. My mother visited him every day. She held his hand. She combed his hair. She spoke softly to him because she wanted him to pass with the comfort of her voice nearby. She suggested that I bring Bo to see Papa, but I could not do it. The thought of Bo seeing Papa in a fragile, deteriorated state terrified me. I knew how sensitive Bo was to suffering. I knew how deeply he absorbed every sound and expression. I also knew my own history with trauma and nightmares, and I feared that Bo would suffer the same way if he saw Papa like that. I wanted to shield him from that pain.

When my mother returned from the nursing home one afternoon with tears in her eyes, I knew immediately what had happened. She walked into the house quietly, set her purse on the table, and sat down without speaking. Her silence told me everything. Papa was gone.

The weight of it crushed me. I felt the air leave my lungs in a way I had never experienced before. Losing a parent figure is difficult at any age, but knowing I now had to explain death to my son was a burden that shook me to my core. My mother looked at me with sorrow carved into her features and whispered, How are you going to tell him?

I did not have an answer. I looked around the house at all the things Papa had touched. His chair. His hat. The medication bottles that still sat on the counter. Every object felt like a reminder of what I had to explain. I walked into the living room where Bo was sitting on the floor watching a movie. The animation flickered on his face, lighting up his eyes. He laughed softly at a scene he had seen many times before. He did not yet know that his world had changed. I stepped back out of the room before he could see my tears.

I sat at the kitchen table and placed my hands flat on the surface. I closed my eyes and looked upward. I had never been someone who asked for signs often, but in that moment, I begged for one. I spoke quietly to God, asking for guidance. I needed a way to help my son understand something that felt impossible to explain. I told God I needed help, not for myself but for Bo, because he deserved a gentle explanation.

As I prayed, something slipped into my thoughts with a clarity that startled me. It was the title of Bo's favorite film, All Dogs Go to Heaven. The words appeared in my mind as clearly as if someone had spoken them aloud. It was not a memory. It felt like an answer. I opened my eyes slowly, absorbing the idea. I could almost feel the relief beginning to form, because for the first time that day, something made sense.

I realized that this movie had been part of Bo's life for years. He understood it. He loved it. He repeated its lines. He connected to its characters. If I explained Papa's passing in a way that tied into what he already understood, he might be able to grasp the idea without fear. I looked at my mother and said, I know how to tell him. She stared at me with surprise, unsure of where the idea came from, but she trusted that I had found something meaningful.

I did not tell Bo immediately. I waited until dinner that evening. The house felt different without Papa's presence. His absence settled over everything like a quiet shadow. As we sat at the table, the weight of what I needed to say pressed against my chest. When we finished our meal, Bo looked at my mother and said, Him, Papa. His voice carried confusion and concern. He wanted to know why Papa was not sitting at the table with us.

My mother looked at me, and I knew it was time.

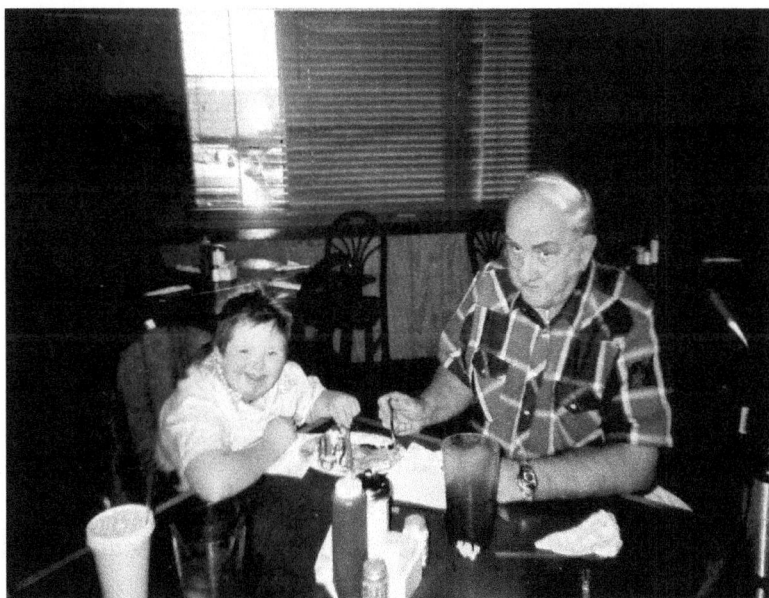

I touched Bo's hand to get his attention. I reminded him of the movie he loved so much. I asked him if he remembered Charlie and Itchy from All Dogs Go to Heaven. He nodded and his face lit up at the mention of the characters. I told him that Papa was with Charlie and Itchy now, in a place where he could fly and run and breathe without hurting. I told him Papa had his wings, just like the characters in the movie.

Bo's eyes widened. His mouth fell open in surprise. He stared at me as if I had told him something extraordinary. Then he repeated the line he loved from the film, the one he always acted out with dramatic flair. He looked right into my eyes and said softly, He can never come back. His tone was not fearful. It was accepting. He understood. In his simple, innocent way, he comprehended the truth that even adults struggle to grasp.

My mother covered her mouth with her hand as tears filled her eyes. I felt a strange mixture of heartbreak and relief. Papa's absence hurt deeply, but hearing Bo understand it without fear brought me comfort. The explanation had reached him in a place beyond logic. He did not need details or graphic descriptions. He only needed a story he trusted.

From that night forward, Bo spoke to Papa in his prayers. Every evening he placed his hands together, whispered his nightly words, and then pulled his hands apart to send his goodbye toward the ceiling. He looked upward and said goodnight, Papa, before ending his prayer with his gentle bye. It became his ritual, a bridge between the life he lived on earth and the love he believed continued in the sky above him.

In the weeks that followed, I watched Bo adjust to the idea that Papa was in a place he could not see but still feel. He asked fewer questions and found comfort in our conversations. He accepted the explanation in a way that only a child with a pure heart could. He did not fear heaven. He did not fear loss. Instead, he believed that Papa was safe and happy, flying with Charlie and Itchy, waiting in a peaceful place beyond the clouds.

What I did not realize was that those conversations about heaven were preparing us both for something far more painful that would come later. At the time, all I wanted was to help my son understand the loss of someone he loved deeply. I wanted to ease his confusion and soften his fear. I did not know that God was using these moments to build a foundation that I would rely on in the darkest chapter of my life.

For now, what mattered was that Bo understood where Papa had gone. He believed with his whole heart that heaven was a place filled with light, animals, and love. He believed that those who went there were not lost. They were simply waiting. And through his innocence, he began to teach me something I had never understood as clearly before. Death does not end love. It simply changes the way love is carried.

In those quiet evenings after Papa passed, I often watched Bo press his small hands together and say his prayers. I listened to his soft voice whispering goodnight. I saw his eyes lift toward the ceiling as if he could see through it. And in those moments, even in the heaviness of grief, I felt a tenderness rise within me. Bo was teaching me how to grieve with faith instead of despair. His belief in heaven was not shaped by fear. It was shaped by love.

I carried that lesson with me, not knowing how much I would need it later. For now, I simply held on to the image of Papa receiving his wings and Bo accepting it with the purity of a child who loved him deeply. That image became the light that guided us through the next chapter of our lives.

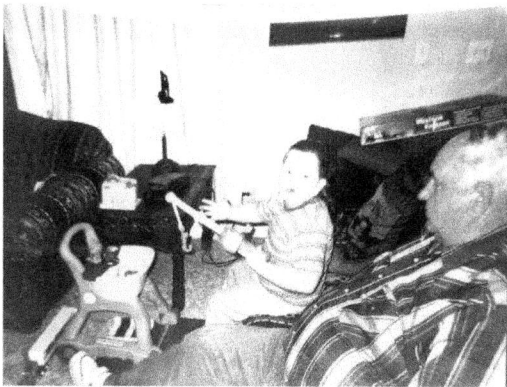

ACTIVITIES

It is okay to feel many different things when someone you love isn't here anymore. You may find it helpful to think about these ideas or share your thoughts in a personal journal.

Reflections for Your Heart:

How I am feeling right now...

The moments when I feel the saddest...

The thing I miss most about Papa...

Something I would tell Papa if I could...

A happy memory I will always have...

CHAPTER 3

TELLING BO ABOUT HEAVEN

The evening after Papa passed away carried a heaviness that pressed against every corner of our home. The air felt still, as if the house itself was holding its breath, waiting for us to speak a truth none of us wanted to say aloud. My mother sat quietly at the table, her grief layered across her face in ways that softened her features and aged her at the same time. I moved through the motions of dinner with a heaviness that I could not shake. Bo sat in his usual spot, humming under his breath as he tapped his fingers against the placemat in a steady rhythm. He looked peaceful on the surface, but I could see the questions rising in his eyes.

The chair at the end of the table, Papa's chair, remained empty. Its absence carried more weight than anything else in the room. Bo's eyes drifted to it again and again. He stared at it with small bursts of confusion, as if waiting for Papa to walk in and sit down with a tired smile. But when the chair remained empty through the entire meal, his curiosity turned into a quiet worry.

His voice broke the silence in the middle of dinner. He looked at my mother and asked simply, Him, Papa. It was not a question he had rehearsed. It was the kind of question that comes from a child searching for something he cannot name. He wanted to know where Papa was and why he had not returned. The sound of his voice made my mother's breath catch, and she looked at me with eyes that begged me to guide us through this moment.

I reached across the table and touched Bo's hand. The warmth of his small palm steadied me. I felt every part of me resisting the weight of what I needed to say, yet I knew it was time. I reminded him softly of the movie he loved so much. I asked him if he remembered Charlie and Itchy in All Dogs Go to Heaven. His face lit up immediately. His memory of that story was perfect. He nodded and whispered the names with affection.

I told him that Papa was in heaven just like the characters in his movie. I explained that Papa could breathe easily now and that he was safe. I described heaven as a place filled with light where no one felt pain. I told him that Papa was happy there. Bo's eyes widened. He looked at me as though I had handed him something precious. Then he repeated the line he cherished from the film. He said, He can never come back. His voice was soft, steady, and completely accepting. There was no fear in his tone, only understanding.

That sentence marked a turning point. It showed that Bo grasped something deeper than I expected. He understood the permanence of heaven in a simple and honest way. His innocence allowed him to absorb a truth that is heavy even for adults. I watched his shoulders relax, as though the answer settled into him like a puzzle piece finally

18

fitting. My mother placed a hand over her heart and lowered her head, moved by the purity of his response.

That night, when it was time for bed, Bo performed his nightly routine with an unusual tenderness. He took his bubble bath, ate his snack, and picked out a movie to fall asleep to. I observed him closely, wondering how the conversation would shape his evening. When we knelt beside his bed for prayers, he folded his hands together with deliberate care. He closed his eyes and whispered his familiar words in a soft voice. When he was finished, he lifted his hands upward and opened them slowly, as if releasing something into the air. It was the gesture he used every night to end his prayers. But that night, he added something new. He looked up toward the ceiling and said, Bye Papa.

The way he said it carried no fear or sadness. It sounded like a message, tender and sincere, sent with the full trust of a child who believes heaven is just above the ceiling, reachable through prayer. I watched him, my heart aching and comforted at the same time. His faith was not complicated. It was built on stories, imagination, and the simple belief that love continues even when someone is gone.

In the days that followed, Bo repeated the gesture every night before bed. He pressed his palms together, whispered his prayers, and lifted his hands at the end. Each time, he looked up and said his small goodbye. His voice never wavered. It carried peace, not fear. His relationship with heaven grew in those evenings. It became a place he spoke to naturally, the same way he spoke to me or to our animals in the yard.

I began to see how deeply stories shaped his understanding of life. Movies were not only entertainment for him. They were windows into ideas that were difficult to explain otherwise. He understood heaven because he understood the narrative of a character who leaves earth for a place that feels safe and joyful. He connected with Charlie and Itchy the way other children connect with friends. They formed a bridge between imagination and faith. They helped him take the idea of heaven and hold it in his hands with confidence instead of fear.

This realization opened something in me. I saw that storytelling had the power to soften even the hardest truths. Watching Bo absorb the concept of death through characters he loved showed me how much comfort a story could offer. It eased his confusion without overwhelming him. It gave him an image of heaven that felt familiar rather than frightening. It gave him a way to stay connected to Papa through ritual and imagination.

There were moments when I watched Bo lift his eyes toward the ceiling and whisper to Papa, and I felt a reflection settle inside me. I recognized that I was learning as much as he was. He taught me that love does not end when someone passes. He taught me that faith can be simple. And he taught me that storytelling can hold the kind of truth that eases grief.

During those evenings, when the house was quiet and Bo's soft voice floated upward, I began to sense something stirring in my spirit. It was a quiet nudge, the kind that speaks without sound. I felt myself returning to the prayer I had whispered on the day Papa passed, the prayer in which I asked God for guidance. The memory of that moment connected to the image of Bo understanding the truth through a story. I began to see that the explanation I gave him was not just an answer. It was a seed. Something had been planted that day, a gentle idea that stories could carry healing.

I did not know it at the time, but this was where the foundation of the book began to form. It took shape in the silence of our home, in the space between loss and understanding, in the innocence of a child who believed that heaven was real because he saw it in a movie he loved. It grew quietly each night as Bo reached toward the sky and sent his little goodbye. It became clearer each time I saw his peace settle in place.

This chapter of our lives taught me that children do not need complicated explanations. They need stories that speak to their hearts. They need images they already trust. They need language that matches their understanding. Bo accepted the truth about heaven because the story connected with his imagination. It allowed him to visualize love continuing in a place he could not see. It allowed him to feel close to Papa even in his absence.

As I watched him embrace this new understanding, I realized that storytelling is not just for children. It is for anyone searching for comfort in the face of loss. It is a bridge between the seen and the unseen. It is a way of carrying hope through grief. And in its quiet, gentle way, it became the first thread in the tapestry of the story I would one day share with the world.

For now, Bo stood at the center of that thread. His prayers rose each night like small lanterns lifting toward the sky. Each one carried love, belief, and innocence. Through him, I learned that heaven could be understood in the simplest way. It could be a place where stories guide the heart and where love continues without end.

ACTIVITIES

Part 1: A Picture of Love

Think about a favorite memory you shared with someone you love. Or, close your eyes and imagine what a peaceful, happy heaven might look like.

Take a separate piece of paper or a special sketchbook and draw that picture. Using your favorite colors, bring that memory or that peaceful place to life. You can keep your drawing in a safe place or hang it up where you can see it every day.

CHAPTER 4

SIGNS FROM ABOVE

There are certain children who seem to live with one foot in this world and one foot in another. Bo was one of them. After Papa passed, he did not cling to grief the way adults often do. He did not focus on absence. Instead, he searched for presence in places most people overlook. His understanding of heaven did not come with fear or finality. It came with curiosity, trust, and a sense of wonder that softened the ache in my own heart. It was during this time that Bo developed a connection with the sky that went beyond anything I had seen before.

Bo had always loved the outdoors, but his fascination with airplanes grew stronger after Papa's passing. Every time he heard the low rumble of an engine overhead, he rushed to the window or ran outside to look upward. He studied each plane with the focus of someone who believed something precious was hidden inside the clouds. When the plane grew small in the distance, he stayed still for a moment, tilting his head as if listening to something beyond hearing.

It did not take long for me to realize why airplanes captured his heart. In his mind, the sky was no longer just a place where birds flew or clouds drifted. It was the home of heaven. It was the doorway to Papa. Every airplane that passed through the sky felt like a bridge between his world and the one he believed Papa lived in. To Bo, airplanes did not simply travel through clouds. They traveled through heaven itself.

One afternoon, while we were riding in the car, an airplane appeared in the sky above us. Bo pressed his face against the window and pointed upward with excitement. He waved his hand as if greeting someone he could see clearly. Then he whispered the words that became one of his signature phrases. He said, Fly, fly. His voice was soft and filled with affection, as though speaking to a friend. I asked him who he was talking to, even though I already sensed the answer forming in his heart. Without hesitation, he said, Papa.

Watching him speak to the sky felt like witnessing a conversation between two worlds. He believed with absolute certainty that Papa flew beside the airplanes, moving through the clouds with ease and joy. He imagined Papa watching over him, waving back, and traveling from one corner of heaven to another through the open air. I listened to him whisper, Fly, fly, and felt my breath catch. His innocence did not weaken the truth. It gave it a purity that felt spiritual.

Bo's understanding of heaven was not built on mourning. It was built on presence. In his mind, Papa was not gone. He was simply above us, living in the sky, watching from the clouds. Bo did not grieve the same way adults do because he did not believe he had lost anything. He believed he still had Papa, only in a different form.

This belief drew him not only toward the sky but also toward cemeteries. Before Papa passed, cemeteries were nothing more than quiet places we drove past. Bo never gave them extra attention. But after that day, the sight of a cemetery made him sit up straighter, as if something inside him recognized a familiar truth. Whenever we visited Papa's resting place, Bo moved with a calm reverence. He walked ahead of me, his steps slow and measured. He approached Papa's grave as though approaching a doorway.

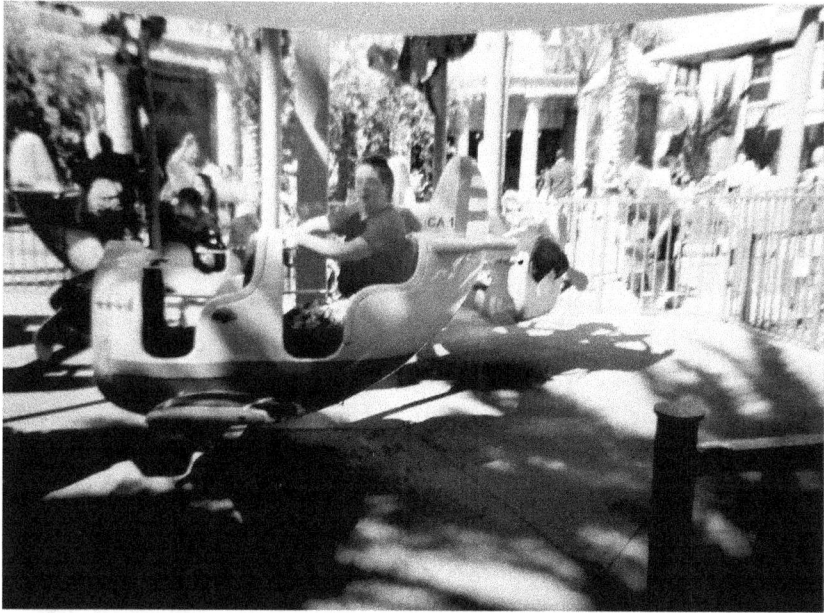

He talked to Papa at the graveside with the same sincerity he used at bedtime when he looked toward the ceiling. He spoke in short sentences filled with tenderness. Sometimes he placed his hand on the headstone. Sometimes he traced the letters of Papa's name with his fingers. Sometimes he closed his eyes and whispered words only he could hear. I never told him what to say. He just knew. In his heart, the cemetery was not a place of sorrow. It was a place where heaven touched the ground for a moment. It felt like a space where the distance between the living and the departed grew thin enough for him to feel connected.

I watched him during those visits and often found myself wondering if children like Bo experience the world differently. They carry an innocence that has not been dulled by cynicism or fear. Their hearts remain open to the possibility that the unseen is just as real as the seen. When Bo stood beside Papa's grave, his face often took on a look of quiet listening. It made me question whether he was imagining his Papa's presence or truly sensing something beyond my understanding.

There were moments when I caught him looking upward with a serene expression. His eyes followed patterns in the clouds with an intensity that made me pause. If a ray of sunlight broke through the sky, he stared at it with awe, as though recognizing a familiar touch. If the wind blew softly, he lifted his chin and closed his eyes, allowing the breeze to wash over him. It was in those small movements that I saw a spiritual sensitivity in him that felt deeper than imagination.

Adults often explain signs from above as coincidences or emotional interpretations. Children like Bo experience them as truth. He did not question whether Papa was near. He simply believed it. He did not doubt whether heaven could be close. He felt it. He did not measure miracles by logic. He listened to the world with a heart open enough to sense what others ignore.

I found myself watching him more closely during this season. Every time he pointed to a plane, every time he waved, every time he whispered Fly, fly, I felt a part of my grief soften. His faith opened a door in my own spirit. I realized that his understanding of heaven did not require explanation or correction. It required protection. It required honoring. His innocence held answers I did not know I needed.

One day, while we were standing at Papa's grave, Bo placed his hand on the headstone and smiled. Not a sad smile. A peaceful one. He tilted his head slightly and whispered something I could not make out. Then he looked up toward the sky, gave his small wave, and whispered Fly. For a moment, the air around us felt still. The sunlight shifted across his face, warm and gentle. I stood beside him, feeling the quiet ache of loss mixed with the strange comfort of his certainty.

As I watched him, a thought entered my mind, quiet but persistent. Was he imagining all of this, or was he seeing something I could not? The world teaches us to trust what we see with our eyes. Children like Bo trust what they feel with their hearts. They are not weighed down by disbelief. They are not limited by logic. They move through life with an innocence that keeps them open to spiritual truths adults often miss.

Standing there, I realized that I did not need to answer that question. It did not matter whether Bo's visions came from imagination or from a sensitivity that reached into places beyond my own sight. What mattered was that these moments brought him peace. They helped him stay connected to someone he loved. They reminded me that heaven does not need to be distant. Sometimes it is as close as a whisper.

Bo's relationship with the sky, airplanes, and cemeteries created a bridge that carried him through grief in a way only he could understand. Through his eyes, loss transformed into presence. Heaven transformed into familiarity. And love transformed into something that lived both above him and beside him.

In those moments, watching him lift his face toward the clouds, I learned again that Bo was a child who lived with a sensitivity that touched the spiritual without hesitation. Whether he imagined Papa flying through the sky or truly sensed him among the clouds, the truth remained the same. His heart knew something mine was only beginning to rediscover.

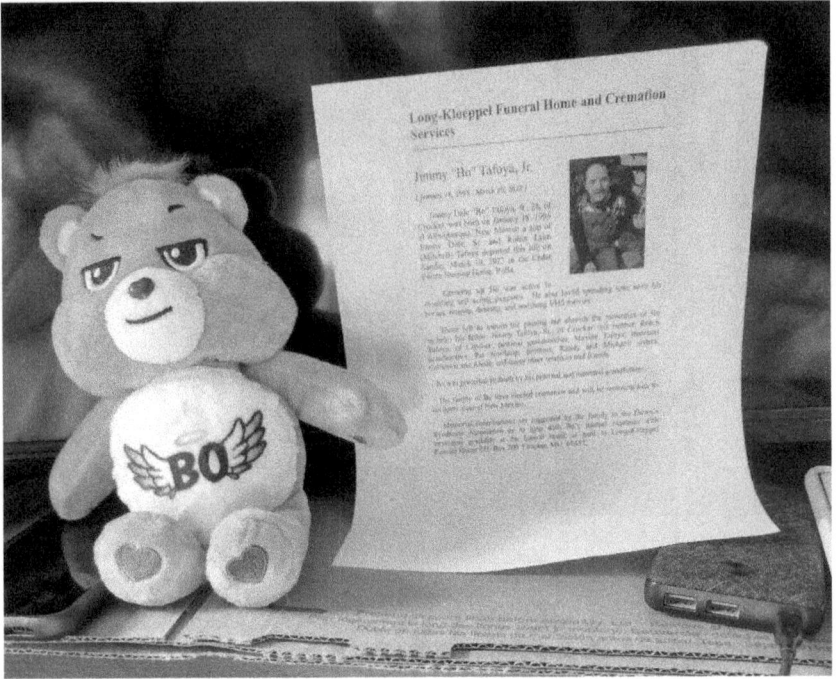

ACTIVITIES

"Bo believed Papa flew with the airplanes."

Sometimes, we feel connected to loved ones through signs—like a butterfly, a certain song, or a ray of sunshine.

Signs of Love: As you look at these images, think about what signs make you feel connected to someone you love. You might even imagine what a guardian angel looks like. If you love to color, you can draw and color these signs on a separate piece of paper to create your own "Sign of Love" collection.

CHAPTER 5

SHADOWS IN MISSOURI

There are seasons in life that arrive quietly, without warning, and settle over everything before you realize how much they have changed. Our move to Missouri happened in the middle of such a season. At first, it felt like a fresh start. A new state. A new home. A chance to rebuild after the loss of Papa and the weight of grief that still lingered in the corners of our days. I wanted to believe the change would bring healing. I wanted to think a new environment would give us room to breathe. But life rarely follows the path you hope for. Missouri became the setting where the first shadows began to gather around us.

The house we moved into sat on a quiet piece of land surrounded by open fields and a long gravel road that stretched into the distance. To someone driving by, it might have looked peaceful. To someone standing in the yard, it might have felt comforting at first. But from the moment we stepped through the door, something in the air felt different. The house was older than it looked from the outside. The floors creaked under the weight of footsteps. The walls held a chill that clung to us no matter how many blankets we used. There were drafty corners that seemed to breathe in the night. And there was a heaviness inside the house that I could not quite explain.

My husband's health had already been slipping before the move. He carried illnesses that doctors struggled to manage, and the stress of relocating only worsened his condition. In the beginning, I tried to stay optimistic. I hoped the quieter environment would help him rest. I hoped the slower pace would ease his pain. Instead, the opposite happened. He grew weaker. His breathing became shallow on some days and labored on others. His strength faded as the weeks passed. I watched him drift in and out of exhaustion like a man fighting a current that kept pulling him under.

Caregiving became a full-time responsibility. I ran the household, managed his needs, and tried to hold everything together while raising a child with disabilities whose behaviors were beginning to shift in unsettling ways. My own isolation grew quickly. The nearest hospital felt far. Friends and family lived too many miles away. The house sat in an area where neighbors kept to themselves. The silence that once seemed peaceful now felt suffocating. There were nights when I cried quietly in the bathroom so neither Bo nor my husband would hear me. I felt trapped between fear and responsibility, trying to stretch myself in ways that no one could sustain.

As my husband's health worsened, I spent more nights sleeping lightly, waking at the slightest sound. The oxygen machine hummed through the dark. The rhythm of his coughing interrupted the stillness of the house. Every time I lay down, I listened for changes in his breathing. I lived in a state of constant alert. Caregiving demands patience and strength, but it also drains those very qualities from you day by day. Missouri became a place where I felt both the weight of my love and the weight of my exhaustion pressing against each other.

In the middle of this strain, Bo began to change. At first the shifts in his behavior were small. He startled at certain sounds he had never reacted to before. He covered his ears more often, even when the room was quiet. He clung to me in a way that felt different than before. His anxiety rose without warning. He cried at noises that never bothered him. He paced through the house as though searching for something he could not name. And when I looked into his eyes, I saw fear rising behind them.

I tried to understand the cause of these changes. At first, I thought it was the move. Children with Down syndrome often struggle with transitions, and leaving the familiarity of home can shake their sense of security. I reassured him gently. I held him longer during bedtime. I stayed close to him whenever he seemed anxious. But the behaviors continued to intensify.

Some nights, he lay in bed wide awake staring at the wall, unable to settle. Other nights, he woke up crying for reasons he could not explain. His fear of sound grew to the point where ordinary noises set him off. If the heater clicked on, he covered his ears. If the floor creaked, he jumped. If I dropped a spoon or closed a cabinet door, he cried out in distress. The house itself seemed to disturb him, as if something in the air unsettled his spirit.

And it did not stop there. His defiance grew in ways that did not match his personality. He started refusing foods he had always loved. He resisted simple routines. He hid behind furniture. He shut down when I tried to redirect him. The child who once moved through life with gentleness and light now carried fear in his body. I felt helpless as I watched him spiral into confusion.

The house did not help. Strange things began happening that only increased my concern. I heard footsteps in empty rooms when no one else was awake. I felt cold drafts that should not have existed. Light flickered unexpectedly. Doors closed softly on their own. I tried to explain these things away. I told myself it was an old house settling. I told myself it was my imagination heightened by stress. But there were moments when the atmosphere in the house thickened in a way that made my skin crawl. I sensed something heavy, something dark, something I could not put a name to.

There were nights when Bo suddenly stopped what he was doing, stared into an empty corner of the room, and backed away slowly as if something frightened him. He clung to me with trembling hands and would not look away from whatever had captured his attention. When I asked him what he saw, he shook his head and buried his face in my chest. These moments grew more frequent, and every one of them left me with a knot in my stomach.

I knew something was wrong, but I did not have the language for it. All I had were observations and instincts, neither of which were enough for doctors. So I took Bo to the hospital, believing that medical professionals could help. Instead, I walked into a maze of confusion, dismissal, and frustration. The hospital staff listened to my concerns with polite expressions but did not take them seriously. They told me children can be sensitive to new environments. They told me behavior changes were normal after a move. They told me to give him time.

When I described the intensity of his fear, they told me he might be acting out for attention. When I explained how the sound sensitivity had escalated rapidly, they suggested sensory overload. When I mentioned the house and its strange atmosphere, they dismissed it entirely. I left each appointment feeling unseen, unheard, and deeply frustrated. I knew my child. I knew when something was off. I knew these behaviors were not typical for him. But the more I tried to advocate for him, the more I felt drowned out by polite, clinical explanations.

I took him to different doctors, hoping for answers, but each visit ended the same way. The medical confusion grew, and with it came a growing sense of helplessness. I watched my son unravel, and no one could tell me why. I felt fear building inside me, fear that something was happening beneath the surface, something we could not detect with tests or diagnoses. The more the professionals minimized my concerns, the more isolated I became.

At home, the shadows seemed to lengthen. My husband's health continued to decline, leaving me physically and emotionally drained. I cooked meals, cleaned the house, managed medications, soothed Bo through anxiety, and struggled through sleepless nights. I tried to keep my voice calm, my spirit steady, and my hope alive, but beneath all that effort, a quiet dread kept growing.

There were moments when I felt watched in the house. Moments when I walked down the hallway and sensed something pressing against the air behind me. Moments when the silence grew too thick, too deep, too unnatural. At times, the hair on my arms stood on end without reason. The atmosphere shifted at unpredictable moments, creating pockets of unease that I could feel physically. I wanted to blame the stress. I wanted to blame exhaustion. But something inside me whispered that this was more than emotional fatigue.

Bo's behavior grew worse in moments when the house felt the heaviest. He cried without warning. He ran into my arms with shaking hands. He refused to enter certain rooms. He refused to sleep in his own bed. The sensitivity to sound became so severe that he began to cry if a door hinge squeaked or if water dripped in the sink. His fear became constant, and my inability to help him tore at me.

Each day I reached for answers. Each day I prayed for a sign. Each day I hoped the shadows would lift. But instead, the sense of foreboding grew. It felt as though something tragic was leaning over our lives, waiting in the doorway. The air in the house grew thicker. The nights grew longer. And Bo's anxiety deepened into a fear that lived in his body.

Looking back, I can see that Missouri was where the first threads of our unraveling began. It was where the light around us dimmed slowly. It was where the weight of the unseen pressed against our daily life until we could not ignore it. It was where I began to realize that the path ahead of us was leading somewhere dark, somewhere I could not predict, somewhere I feared I would not be prepared for.

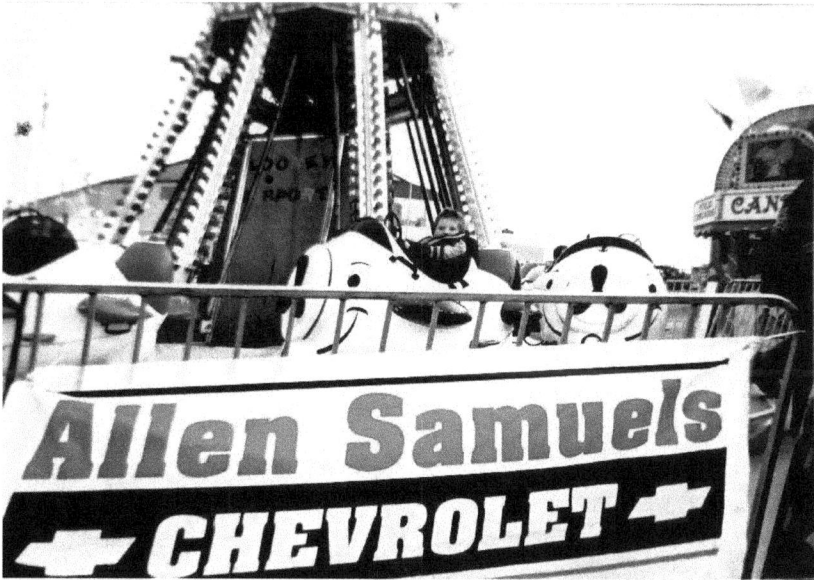

At the time, all I knew was that something was coming. Something I could feel but not name. Something that hovered at the edge of our days, waiting for its moment to break through. And though I tried to carry strength for my son and my husband, a quiet truth settled inside me.

The shadows in Missouri were not just around us.

They were coming for us.

ACTIVITIES

Part 1: My Feelings Are Welcome

Bo felt scared and couldn't explain why. It is important to remember that it is okay to have big feelings.

Look at the faces below. Do you recognize any of these feelings? You might feel sad, anxious, scared, angry, or even a little confused sometimes. All of these feelings are welcome. You can talk about these feelings with someone you trust or even use them as a guide to draw how you feel on a separate piece of paper.

CHAPTER 6
THE NIGHT EVERYTHING CHANGED

There are nights that enter a person's life with such force that they never leave. Nights that tear the world apart in a single blow and scatter every piece of normal life across a landscape you never recover from. For us, that night arrived in March 2023, when every warning sign that had been gathering in Missouri collided at once. The weeks leading up to it were filled with confusion, fear, exhaustion, and an unraveling that none of us saw coming until it was too late.

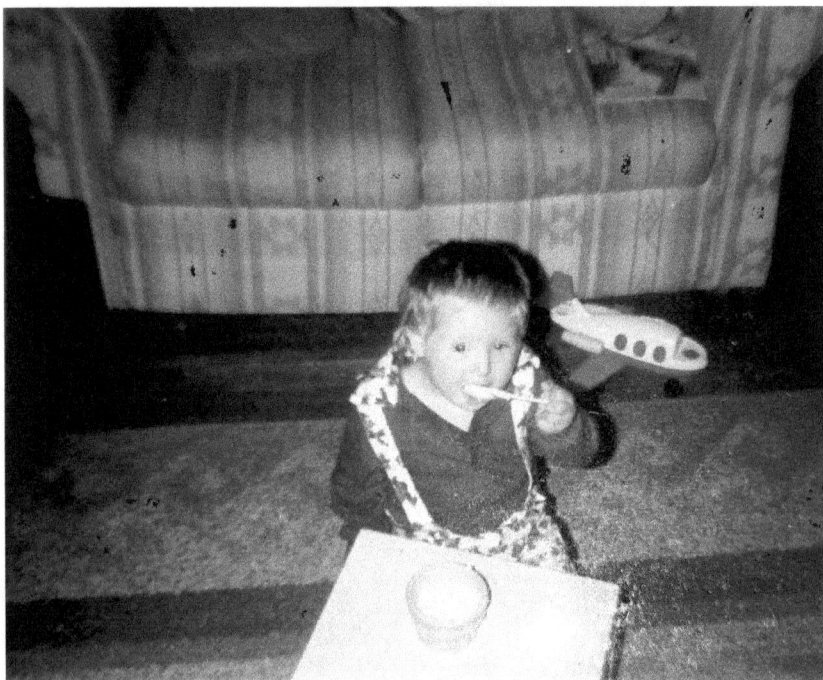

Bo had already been changing. His fear had grown. His anxiety had sharpened. His sensitivity to sound had become overwhelming. But the shift that happened during those days was unlike anything we had faced before. The child who had once been gentle, affectionate, and tender began experiencing sudden violent outbursts that were completely out of character. They appeared without warning, as if something inside him was fighting a battle he could not understand.

At first, the outbursts lasted only a few moments. He began throwing things on the floor and at me. He tore heaters off the wall and broke the television in his frustration, and the chaos frightened both of us. Bo did not turn on his dog. The dog became upset when he saw the outbursts and the confusion caused him to react in a way he never had before. In that moment the dog turned on me, something completely out of character for a border collie. He hurt me badly and the shock of it left me shaken. It frustrated me and frightened me to see a loving animal behave this way, especially in front of my son. I knew I had to make a decision I never wanted to face. For the safety of both myself and Bo, I made the heartbreaking choice to put the dog down. This dog had been Bo's best friend from the time he was six weeks old, sleeping beside him, following him everywhere, and loving him with a devotion that made this loss even harder to bear.

Making the decision to put the dog down felt like a wound layered on top of every other wound we were already carrying. Bo adored that dog. They had grown up together. They had shared quiet afternoons and playful mornings. But Bo's sudden shift in behavior, combined with the dog's fear, created a dangerous situation. I sat with the dog in the final moments and cried. It was another loss in a year already too full of grief. I knew that explaining this to Bo would be nearly impossible. His understanding of death was gentle and childlike, shaped by the stories he loved. But this loss was immediate, confusing, and wrapped in pain.

When I told him the dog was gone, he looked at me with wide eyes that filled quickly with tears. He asked where the dog had gone. I told him the truth as gently as I could. I said Nana was in heaven with Papa. In heaven with all dogs go to heaven with charlie and itchy. He held on to that explanation with a trembling acceptance, but the sadness in his eyes lingered. Another piece of his world had been taken from him.

The loss of the dog seemed to push Bo further into distress. His anxiety intensified. His outbursts became more frequent. I reached out to the hospital again and again, desperate for answers, desperate for support, desperate for someone to see the urgency of what was happening. What I received instead was dismissal, confusion, and a lack of understanding that made everything worse. They treated his behavior as simple defiance. They treated my concerns as exaggeration. They saw none of the terror unfolding in our home.

Then came the night everything changed.

December 25th 2022 arrived like a breaking point. Bo's behavior escalated into chaos that no parent should ever face alone. He screamed at sounds that did not exist. He threw objects across the room. He curled into a ball on the floor, shaking and covering his ears. His breathing grew fast and shallow. His eyes darted around as if seeing something none of us could see. I held him, trying to soothe him, but he thrashed in fear.

December 25th, 22nd, Christmas Day, was the last time I saw my son. After the fire department came, the police and ambulance arrived as well. Bo had become so used to these people showing up that he reacted almost as if it were routine. Every time a behavior issue happened, they came, and he responded in a familiar pattern. It was like he became a different child the moment they walked through the door. Before they arrived he was overwhelmed and out of control, but once they stepped inside the house he shifted into what looked like his normal self. The contrast was so noticeable that it felt as if he were two different children depending on who stood in front of him.

I was his mom and his caregiver at the same time. That Christmas evening the ambulance took him, and he was already so used to going since October that it felt like a routine to him. They would come and take him to help him get better, and we usually brought him home the same day. But this time was different. He walked out of the house as if he were going to a store. I said I love you as loudly as I could so he would hear me, but he did not respond. He just kept walking toward the ambulance without looking back at me. My husband was not home, and the whole moment felt unreal. It was like he was not himself. He loved his kisses and his hugs every day, yet that day I did not get to give him a kiss, I did not get to give him a hug, and I did not get to tell him Mommy loves you and I will be right there. The little boy walking out that door did not feel like my same baby, and the sight of it tore me apart. I cried and wondered what I had done wrong. I believed I was a good parent and did everything I could. I taught him so much and he was not only my son, he was my buddy. Anyone who knew us would say we were inseparable, two peas in a pod. No one cared and no one showed compassion. The whole scene felt like something from a horror movie.

They placed him in a hospital where he did not know anyone. Where he did not understand the rules. Where he could not communicate the way he needed to. Where people did not know how to comfort him. Where he was surrounded by strangers in a sterile environment that felt nothing like home.

That night, I called him on the phone. His voice was broken and small. He cried with such force that I had to hold the phone away from my ear. He begged for me. He said Mama again and again. I begged the staff to let me see him. They refused. I asked for updates. They gave none. I tried to explain his needs. They brushed me aside. The system that was supposed to protect him treated him like a number on a list.

March 19th. The phone rang, and when I answered, my world split into before and after. A cold voice on the other end told me the words no mother should ever hear. They told me Bo had died in the night. They said it with a tone that carried no grief, no humanity, and no understanding of what they had destroyed.

I dropped the phone. I could not breathe. I could not think. I could not process the words. The room spun around me as my legs gave out. I felt a scream rise from the deepest part of my body, a sound filled with anguish that shattered the air. My baby was gone. Not at home. Not in my arms. Not surrounded by love. But in a cold facility where he was afraid, alone, and unheard.

They did not tell me the exact cause of his death. All I was told was that he was unresponsive, and that they had spoken to him before it happened. That Friday it felt like they knew more, but they would not tell me anything. No one there offered even a single word of compassion. No one said they were sorry for what happened to me or to him. The silence and the lack of care made the pain even heavier.

Everything that had been unraveling in Missouri reached its breaking point in that single moment. The outbursts. The fear. The confusion. The warnings. The desperation. The pleas for help. It all led to the phone call that tore my world apart.

That night changed everything. It became the line that separated who I was from who I was forced to become. And it marked the beginning of a grief that would follow me into every day that came after.

ACTIVITIES

A Moment of Reflection

Sometimes, sharing our hardest moments helps us heal. Take a quiet moment to think about a time that felt very difficult for you.

In your personal journal or on a separate piece of paper, you might want to complete this sentence: **"My hardest moment was when..."**

Heart Reflection: You can also draw a heart in your journal. Some people find it helpful to shade in a part of that heart to show how much they were hurting that day. Looking at your heart can remind you of how brave you are for carrying those big feelings.

CHAPTER 7
A HEART THAT STOPPED TWICE

There are moments in life that feel too heavy for the human heart to hold. Moments that strike with such force that every breath afterward becomes a struggle. The morning I learned Bo was gone will remain etched into my memory for as long as I live, but the pain did not end with that call. It was only the beginning. The hours that followed required a strength I did not possess, yet somehow I moved through them because I had no choice. Grief does not pause for breath. It does not wait for you to gather yourself. It hits in waves, relentless and unforgiving.

The first wave came when I had to tell my husband that our son was dead.

Our boy is gone....!!!

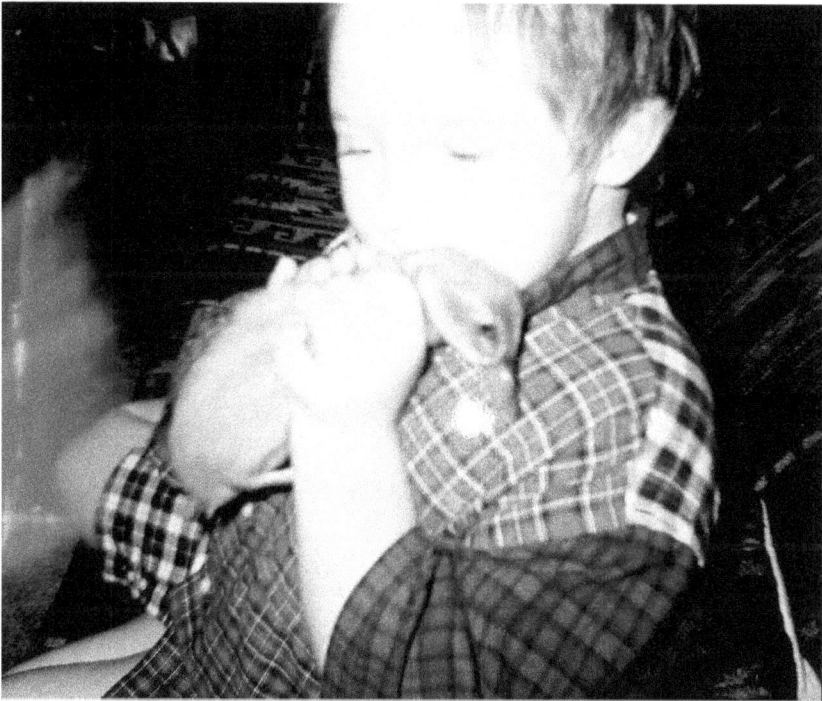

His dad was in the ICU at another hospital having heart surgery, and I had to tell him the moment I found out over the phone. It was one of the hardest things I ever had to do. I was yelling, crying, and screaming because the pain was too much, and he cried too. He was in shock and I had no one there to comfort me or guide me through what I needed to tell him. I asked him about the burial, even though it felt impossible to bring it up. The funeral home was not compassionate at all. They wanted answers that same evening. I was torn apart, and then he told me we did not have burial insurance for him or for me. Keep in mind this was a retired military man who had always taken care of everything. I trusted him to have things in order, and hearing that only made my anxiety and temper worse. Things got loud and I hung up even more upset, knowing I still had to make a decision between cremation and a casket under the circumstances. We had planned on moving back to New Mexico before all the health problems began, so I chose cremation because the cost of a casket and transportation was too much. I had to call the funeral home and explain that our finances were not good. I started a GoFundMe page and hoped people would help. I was grateful for everyone who donated, including strangers and people who knew my son and wanted to support us. Some of them had never even met him, yet they still helped in ways I will never forget. Even with the help, when I left Missouri I still owed money to the funeral home. I told myself the hardest part was burying my son and then having to bury my husband. Since my son had been in state custody, I believed the state should pay the remaining balance. I had to pay two thousand five hundred dollars before they would release his ashes to me. The state only needed to cover five hundred, but instead of paying it, they sent me a bill two years later saying I owed the rest plus interest. It felt unfair that they took my child, refused to listen to me, and then left me to handle every part of the arrangements alone. I am still dealing with that bill today.

I found myself alone in a strange house trying to plan a funeral for my child and my husband. I had to speak with officials who treated my grief like a bureaucratic process. Every conversation felt like a knife twisting deeper into me.

And in the middle of all this, the house itself became a reminder of everything we had lost. Every room held echoes of Bo. His toys. His clothes. His movies. His blankets folded neatly on a shelf. His laughter still seemed to linger in the air, as if refusing to leave. Walking through that house felt like walking through a memory I could not escape. I packed boxes with shaking hands. I sorted through his things in a daze, unsure of how to separate what to keep from what to let go. Grief had carved itself into every corner, and I felt myself drowning in it.

While planning husband's and son's funeral, I also had to decide what to do with the house. There was no way I could stay in Missouri. Every day there felt like standing in the ruins of a life that had been shattered. So I prepared to sell it, even though the process felt impossible. I made calls to realtors. I handled paperwork. I sorted items for storage. I felt like I was moving through thick fog, unable to see anything clearly. My mind was numb, my heart shattered, and my strength depleted.

His health had been deteriorating for months, but losing Bo broke something inside him that his body could not recover from. His passing happened quietly, without warning, while I was still fighting to process the first loss. It was as if the weight of grief had been too much for his heart to bear.

My heart had stopped once the day I learned Bo was gone. It stopped again when I realized my husband had left this world too. Two losses in three weeks. Two people I loved more than anything. Two pieces of my life gone before I could catch my breath. The house fell into a silence so deep that even the sound of my own breathing felt out of place.

The days that followed were a blur. Grief took over every part of my life, but I still had responsibilities to handle. I had to arrange two funerals in less than a month. I had to speak with funeral directors. I had to sign more papers. I had to manage bills that arrived without mercy. Cremation costs. Transportation fees. Legal documents that required signatures even though my hands trembled uncontrollably. Death does not pause for grief. It demands tasks. It demands decisions. It demands money. It demands practicality at a time when the heart can barely function.

They wrote on his death certificate that the cause of death was Down syndrome. You do not die from Down syndrome. He had it, but it is not an illness. It is a syndrome, and seeing that listed as the reason he died weighed heavily on my heart. I wanted a test done to prove that my son had overdosed and that what happened to him was their fault. They did not do it. They were in a hurry to cremate him, in a hurry to finish everything without giving me the chance to ask questions or get the answers I needed. I did not even get to see my son's body before the cremation. He was not at the funeral home where they said he would be, and that made everything even harder. I never got to see him one last time. I never got to hug him, kiss him, or say goodbye.

I found myself trapped in legal struggles I never wanted to face. I made countless phone calls. I sat on hold for hours. I repeated my story over and over to people who treated it like routine. Every conversation felt like reliving the trauma. I fought for corrections. I fought for answers. I fought for accountability. I fought for dignity for a child who had been taken from me by a system that had not protected him.

In the midst of all this, my faith began to tremble. I had always believed in God. I had always trusted that even in the darkest moments, He walked beside us. But grief can shake even the strongest foundations. I found myself asking questions I never thought I would ask. Why? Why us? Why now? Why my child? Why my husband? Why did everything fall apart at once? Why did God allow darkness to fall so heavily on a family already struggling?

There were days when I could not pray. Days when I felt abandoned. Days when I wondered if God had turned His face from me. The weight of grief pressed against my spirit until I questioned everything I had ever believed. I searched for purpose in the suffering, but I could not find any. I searched for meaning in the loss, but the pain drowned out every answer. I searched for light, but all I felt was darkness.

I tried to keep moving because I had no choice. I packed the house, scheduled movers, and prepared to leave Missouri behind. I forced myself to rise each morning even though my body felt heavy with sorrow. I did paperwork. I handled bills. I answered calls. But inside, I was crumbling. My heart had stopped twice, once for my son and once for my husband, and I did not know how to make it beat again with anything that resembled hope.

Looking back, I do not know how I survived those weeks. The grief was too heavy. The responsibilities were too overwhelming. The loneliness was too deep. Yet somehow, despite everything, I kept going. Maybe it was instinct. Maybe it was the faintest thread of faith still clinging to my spirit. Maybe it was the memory of Bo's innocence and the belief that he would not want me to give up. Whatever it was, it carried me through the darkest season of my life.

Missouri became the place where everything fell apart. The place where I lost my child. The place where I lost my husband. The place where I faced grief that nearly destroyed me. And yet it was also the place where the first seeds of healing were planted, buried deep beneath the pain, waiting for a time when I could breathe again.

When I got back to New Mexico, I had to take care of my mom, and it was not easy because she was grieving the loss of her grandson. He was supposed to be coming back home with me. My mom could not handle the way he died. She felt it was cruel and inhumane. She spoke to him every day up until the day he passed, and losing him took a heavy toll on her. She loved him deeply, and he was her everything. He loved her the same way, and she taught him so much. Then her day came on October first of twenty twenty four when she passed away. I was faced with even more loss and more grief to carry. Three people in two years had passed away, and now I have to teach myself how to start over and grieve in my own time.

ACTIVITIES

Finding What Remains

Grief can feel like losing a piece of our world, but even in loss, there are things we still carry in our hearts. Consider these two thoughts:

- **Something I have lost is...**
- **Something I still have is...**

A Creative Reflection: If you have a separate notebook or a piece of paper, you might like to draw two circles. You can use one circle to represent your loss and the other to represent what remains. You can use different colors or patterns to show how each circle feels to you. Looking at these two circles together can help you see that love and memory are always with you.

CHAPTER 8
WHEN ANGELS WEEP

In the weeks following the deaths of my son and my husband, grief became my constant companion, but it was not the only weight pressing against me. A second struggle rose quickly, one I never imagined I would have to face while still gasping for breath beneath the weight of loss. It was the battle against a system that had failed Bo so completely. A system that claimed to protect vulnerable children but treated my son like a case file instead of a human life. A system that took him from my arms, dismissed my warnings, ignored his needs, and returned him to me only through a phone call that shattered my heart forever.

When the shock began to lift just enough for me to think again, anger entered the grief. It did not arrive as rage but as a quiet determination that grew slowly, gathering strength each day. I knew my son had died under state care. I knew an overdose had taken his life. I knew mistakes had been made, decisions mishandled, warnings ignored, and protocols neglected. I knew that what happened to Bo was not simply tragic. It was wrongful.

I wanted answers. I needed them. I needed to understand what happened in those final hours. I needed to know how a child who had just been taken from his home could die so quickly under the supervision of trained professionals. I needed the truth, not the rehearsed lines and vague statements they offered. So I began the process of seeking legal help, believing that justice was possible if I could find someone willing to fight alongside me.

The first lawyer I contacted listened politely but declined the case. He said it was complicated. He said the state was difficult to fight. He said the odds were slim. The second lawyer told me something similar. The third one did not even allow me to finish the story before explaining that wrongful death under state care was nearly impossible to win. Every rejection felt like a door slamming in my face. Each one reminded me how powerless families can become when institutions close ranks to protect themselves.

I continued searching. I continued calling. I continued telling my son's story to people who responded with rehearsed sympathy and practiced caution. Many listened, but few were willing to act. They said the state held immunity. They said the legal path was long and expensive. They said the burden of proof was too heavy. I understood the risks, but I could not accept silence. I could not accept the idea that my son's death would be brushed aside as a bureaucratic inconvenience.

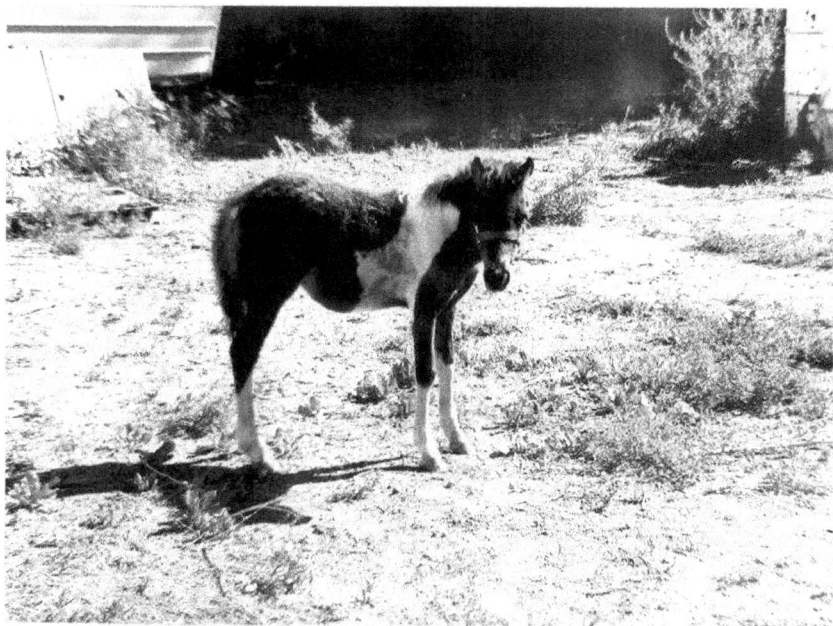

Each rejection deepened my sorrow, but it also ignited a fire inside me. I realized I was battling more than grief. I was battling a system that protected itself better than it protected the children in its care. A system that failed to see Bo as a person with a life worth fighting for. A system that treated his death as a footnote rather than an outrage.

The moral and emotional implications of his wrongful death weighed heavily on my spirit. It was not just that Bo had died. It was how he had died. It was where he had died. It was the circumstances that led to his final moments. A child with special needs had been taken from his safe space, placed in a facility that did not understand him, and left vulnerable to danger that could have been prevented. That truth haunted me.

I wrestled with the reality that I had trusted the wrong people. I wrestled with the guilt of believing their promises of safety. I wrestled with the unbearable fact that my son's last night on earth had been filled with fear and confusion instead of comfort. Even though I knew none of this was my fault, grief has a way of twisting logic until you blame yourself for things you could never have stopped.

As I navigated the maze of bureaucracy, I felt myself confronting deep questions about human failure, institutional neglect, and the consequences of ignoring vulnerable lives. The more I learned, the clearer it became that my son's story was not an isolated tragedy. There were others. Other children harmed. Other families silenced. Other lives dismissed by the very people tasked with protecting them.

This realization forced me to see the world differently. Painfully. Honestly. I understood that systems can fail. I understood that professionals can overlook warning signs. I understood that policies can be written with good intentions but executed with indifference. I understood that accountability is often avoided rather than embraced. The weight of that truth was overwhelming.

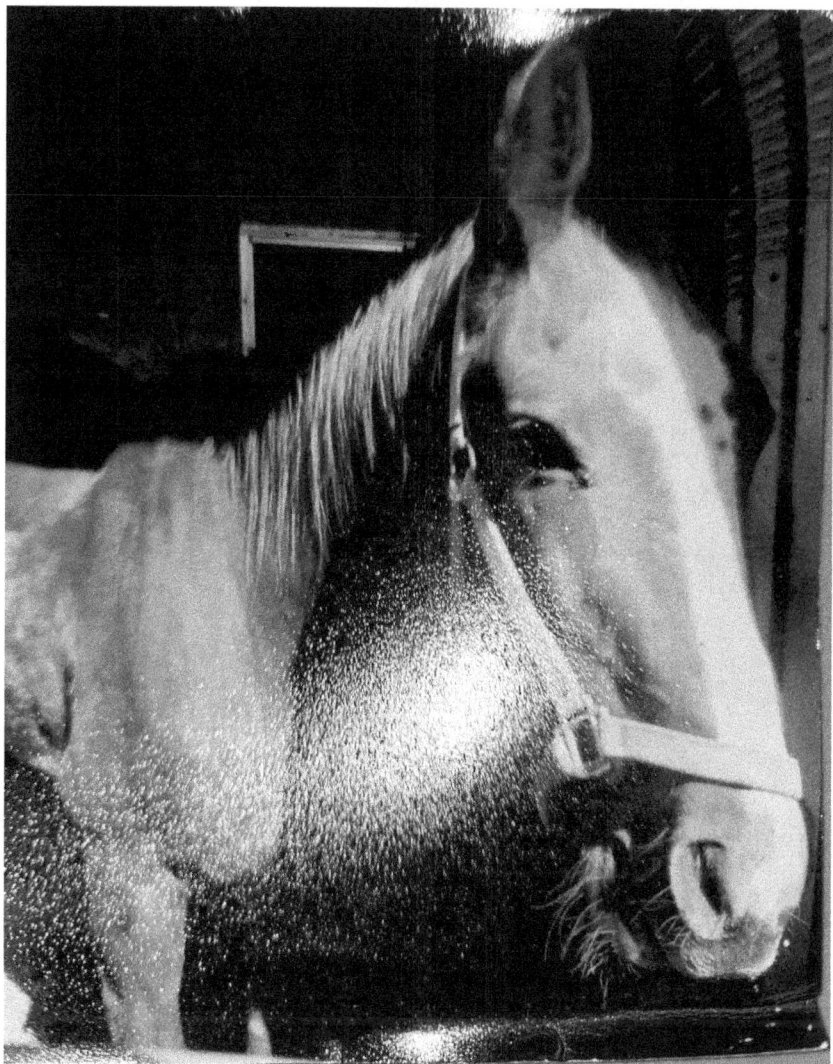

But in the midst of that heaviness, something began to shift inside me. The grief that had once drowned me began to take a new shape. I still cried every day. I still felt the ache of loss in every breath. I still reached for my son's memory with trembling hands. But beneath the pain, a new sense of purpose started to awaken. It was small at first, like a whisper in the quiet moments. A thought that returned again and again, growing stronger each time.

Tell his story.

At first, I resisted the idea. I was still raw from the trauma. Still shattered from losing my son, my husband and my mom. Still fighting legal battles that felt impossible to win. But the whisper persisted. Tell his story. Each time I replayed Bo's life in my mind, each time I remembered his innocence, his kindness, his faith, his fascination with the sky, I felt the whisper pushing deeper.

The truth became impossible to ignore. Telling his story was not just about grief. It was not just about memory. It was about justice. It was about making sure his life meant something beyond the tragedy. It was about ensuring that no other child was taken from their home and left unprotected. It was about honoring the boy who loved airplanes, prayers, animals, movies his family and the sky with his whole heart.

The more I reflected, the more I realized that Bo's story had the power to awaken change. His innocence could soften hearts. His suffering could open eyes. His death could expose the failures of a system that desperately needed accountability. Sharing his journey could help others understand the reality of raising a vulnerable child in a world not built to protect them.

Slowly, grief transformed into mission.

Not because the pain lessened, but because the **LOVE** grew stronger. **LOVE** can become fuel when pain threatens to consume you. **LOVE** can become a compass when life leaves you lost. **LOVE** can become a shield when injustice threatens to silence the truth.

As I stood amid paperwork, unanswered questions, and the echoes of the three losses that had reshaped my life, I made a promise to myself and to my son.

His story would not end in silence.

I would speak for him.

I would fight for him.

I would honor him.

I would carry him forward through every word I wrote.

Grief had broken me open, but from the broken pieces came a purpose strong enough to hold the weight of his memory. This mission did not erase the pain, but it gave it direction. It gave it shape. It gave it a place to go.

Bo's life deserved truth.

Bo's death demanded justice.

And my heart, though shattered, refused to let him fade into the shadows.

Through telling his story, I found a way to keep him alive in this world. Through the pages of this book, his spirit continues to rise, just as he believed Papa rose into the sky. And maybe, somewhere in the space between earth and heaven, an angel who once loved life looks up and smiles, knowing his story is finally being told.

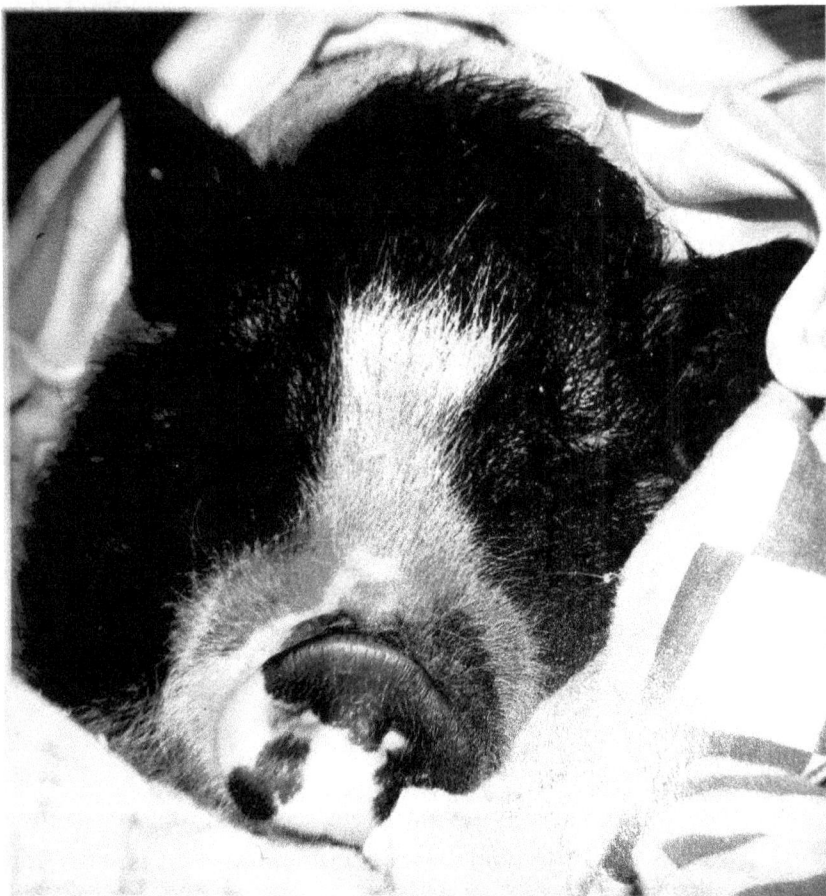

ACTIVITIES

A Message from the Heart

Sometimes, when we are going through something very hard, there is a truth we want the whole world to understand. It can be powerful to say it out loud or hold it in your mind.

Take a moment to think about this: What is one thing you wish people knew about how you are feeling or what you are going through?

If you are using a journal, you might want to begin with the words: "People need to know that..."

CHAPTER 9

GUARDIANS AMONG US

After losing my son, husband and my mom the world felt strangely quiet, as if everything had been drained of color. Days blended together, and nights stretched long, filled with thoughts that refused to rest. Grief had settled into every corner of my life, and even the simplest tasks felt heavy. I often wondered how a single heart could carry so much pain without breaking completely. Yet in the middle of that darkness, something unexpected began to unfold. Small moments, gentle presences, and quiet blessings began appearing in ways I could not ignore. They were subtle at first, almost easy to dismiss, but they became steady reminders that even in the deepest sorrow, help can arrive in forms we never anticipate.

One of the first signs came in the shape of a woman I had never met before. She was the hospice nurse assigned to check on me after my husband passed. I expected a brief, clinical visit, perhaps a few questions and a polite goodbye. Instead, she became a lifeline in a moment when I had almost nothing left to hold onto.

Her compassion felt different from the rehearsed sympathy I had grown used to. She listened without rushing. When she realized how alone I was in that state, something shifted in her voice.

She became more than a nurse that day. She became a guardian. She brought warmth into a home that had felt cold since the moment my husband took his last breath. Her kindness was not merely a part of her job. It was a gift she chose to give. I sometimes wondered how she sensed exactly what I needed before I said anything. Her presence reminded me that even strangers can carry light into the darkest places.

Not long after, another guardian entered my life in a completely different form. He did not speak, but his presence spoke volumes. He was a dog, one whose spirit seemed to understand sorrow without needing explanations. From the moment he came home with me, he stayed close, watching me as if he knew my heart had been shattered. When I cried, he placed his head on my lap. When I sat in silence, he curled beside me. When grief pushed me to the point of breaking, he nudged my hand gently until I felt grounded again.

There were days when the tears came without warning, and I felt the familiar wave of loss press against my chest. Every time, without fail, he appeared at my side. His eyes were filled with a depth that felt almost human, as if he recognized the weight I carried. It amazed me how an animal could sense emotions so clearly. He walked with me through the empty rooms of the house, sat beside me during long nights, and rested his head on my shoulder whenever I felt I could not breathe. His presence brought comfort in a way words never could.

It was as if he had been sent to remind me I was not completely alone. He did not fix my grief, but he softened it. He made the silence less harsh. He offered companionship in moments when I felt invisible to the rest of the world. Animals have a way of seeing pain without judgment, of offering love without conditions. He became a quiet healer, guiding me back to a place where hope could begin to grow again.

As time passed, I started noticing small moments of grace appearing in ways I had never expected. A kind word from a neighbor. A warm smile from a cashier. A moment of sunlight breaking through a cloudy day. A quiet morning when the air felt peaceful for the first time in months. These were not dramatic miracles. They were simple, gentle reminders that sorrow does not erase goodness. Grief had narrowed my world, but these small gifts began widening it again.

Each moment felt like a whisper of encouragement. A reminder that healing does not come all at once. It arrives in pieces, through people and animals and fleeting moments that touch the heart in ways we cannot fully explain. I started to understand that angels are not always the winged beings we imagine in stories. Sometimes they are nurses who sit beside us in silence. Sometimes they are dogs who sense our pain before we speak. Sometimes they are strangers whose kindness appears at the exact moment we feel we cannot bear another ounce of sorrow.

As these realizations unfolded, something shifted inside me. The heavy fog that had surrounded my spirit began to lift, even if just slightly. I started to feel hints of divine purpose again, not in large revelations but in gentle reminders that I was still being guided. The losses I endured had left deep wounds, but these signs of grace helped me believe that my story was not over. Healing did not erase the past, but it allowed me to see a future shaped by love instead of only pain.

One tender moment at a time, my heart began to open again. One kind gesture at a time, my faith began to rise again. One quiet blessing at a time, I started to believe that God had not abandoned me. He had surrounded me with guardians, each one carrying a piece of the strength I needed. They arrived in human hands, in soft fur, and in moments of peace that felt too perfectly timed to be coincidence.

Through them, I learned an important truth: angels walk among us. They do not always appear in bright light or dramatic visions. Sometimes they arrive in everyday forms, offering comfort, guidance, and reminders that we are never as alone as we feel. These guardians helped me find my way back to purpose, slowly but surely. They helped me breathe again. They helped me see that even in seasons of unimaginable loss, grace continues to flow.

Their presence reminded me that love continues, even after death. Compassion continues, even after heartbreak. Hope continues, even when the world feels shattered. And through that truth, I began to believe that Bo my husband and my mom were still watching over me, still guiding me, still sending reminders from a place where angels dance in the sky.

ACTIVITIES

Honoring Your Guardian

A guardian can be a special person, a beloved pet, or even a symbol that makes you feel safe and watched over. Thinking about who or what protects your heart can bring a sense of peace.

In your journal, you may want to reflect on this: "My guardian was special because..."

A Creative Idea: On a separate piece of paper or in your sketchbook, try creating a picture of your guardian. You can use simple shapes— like circles, triangles, or hearts—to build a drawing of the person, pet, or symbol that represents safety and love to you.

CHAPTER 10

DANCING IN THE SKY

In the quiet moments of my life now, I often find myself returning to the memories of Bo as a little boy sitting beside me, asking questions that stretched far beyond his years. I remember the nights when he looked up at the ceiling and asked where Papa went. I remember how I tried to explain heaven to him in simple words, telling him that loved ones never really leave. I remember the way he listened with wide eyes, absorbing every detail as if he were building a picture in his mind. I did not know then that those conversations were preparing me for a future I never wanted to face. I did not know that the lessons I taught him about heaven would become the lessons I would lean on to survive his passing.

Life has a way of coming full circle, sometimes in heartbreaking ways. I once explained death to my child in a way that would not frighten him. I told him heaven was a place filled with light, a place where no one hurts and no one cries. I told him Papa was safe, happy, watching over us. I told him love does not end when a person leaves the earth. Love is a bond that stretches across distance and time, stronger than anything life can break. Back then, I spoke those words to comfort him. Today, I speak them to comfort myself.

As I move forward through the weight of everything that has happened, I find myself holding on to the belief that love continues beyond sight. It changes shape, but it does not disappear. It becomes memory, presence, guidance, and quiet reminders. It becomes the warmth that settles over me on mornings when the world feels too heavy. It becomes the whisper of peace I feel when I look at the sky. It becomes the connection that refuses to fade no matter how much time passes.

There are days when I close my eyes and imagine where Bo is now. I see him free from every struggle he faced in this world. I see him moving without fear, without pain, without limitations. I see him surrounded by every animal he loved, running through fields of endless space where nothing can harm him. I imagine him looking up, reaching toward the clouds, laughing with the kind of joy only children understand. In my heart, I see him dancing in the sky.

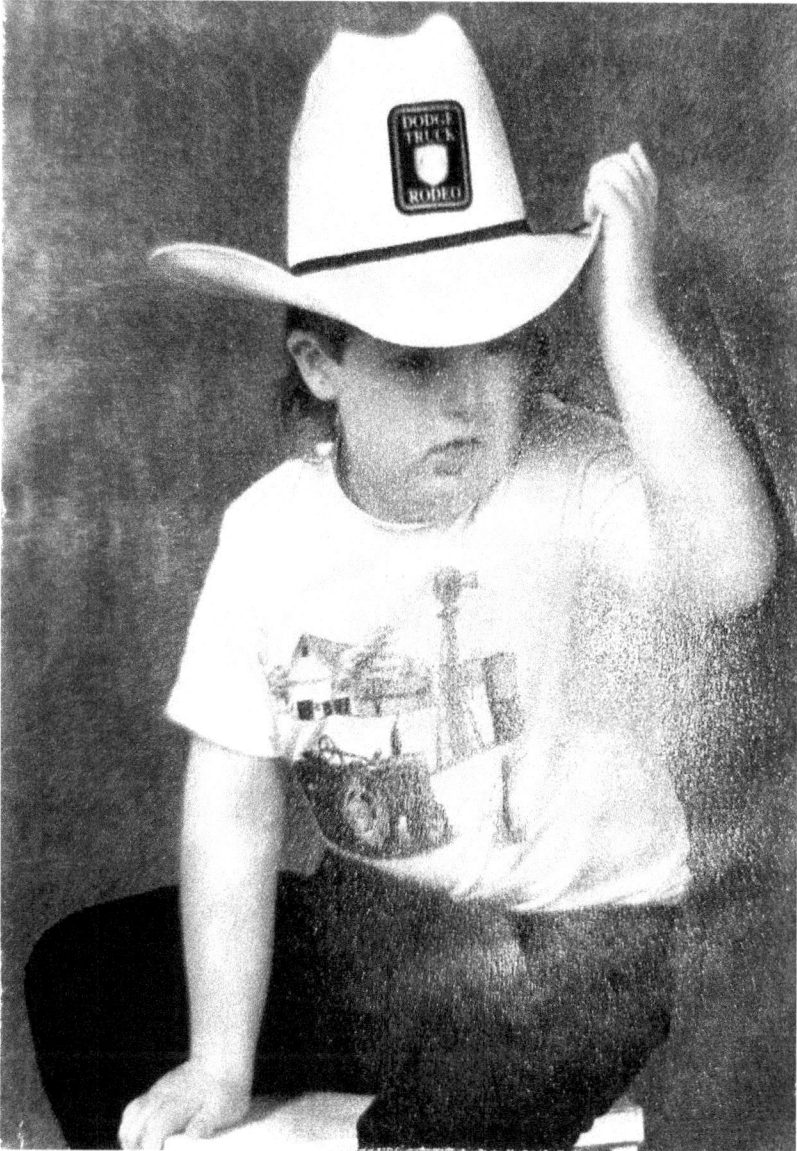

The picture is clear. He is not alone. He is with his Papa, the one he prayed for each night before bed. He is with the pets he cherished. He is with loved ones who left this earth long before he did. They are all together now, wrapped in peace I cannot yet imagine. When I think of them, I feel a softness settle over my spirit. It does not erase the grief, but it gives it purpose. It gives it hope. It gives it meaning.

Through this journey, I have come to understand something profound. Heaven is not far away. It is not a distant place unreachable by the living. It is closer than we think. It is felt in the love that lingers long after a person has left. It is found in the memories that rise unexpectedly and bring comfort instead of pain. It is carried in the unseen guidance that shapes our days without us realizing it. Heaven is the bond that remains unbroken.

This message is not only for parents who have lost children. It is for every child who faces the unknown and every adult who struggles to explain it. It is for every heart that has been shattered by loss and every soul that seeks healing. The truth I hold now is simple but powerful. Love never leaves. It remains in the spaces between breaths, in the dreams that feel like visits, in the gentle signs that arrive when we need them most. Heaven is the continuation of love, not the end of it.

One day, I believe we will all be together again under the same sky. One day, the separation that feels so unbearable now will become a moment in an eternal story. One day, Bo will reach for my hand again, and we will dance with the same joy he imagined when he looked at airplanes soaring above him. Until that day comes, I carry him with me in every step I take. I honor him through the life I continue to build. I share his story so his spirit never fades from this world.

Bo taught me more about love, faith, and perseverance than any book or lesson could. His innocence, kindness, and imagination shaped me in ways I am still discovering. Even now, his presence guides me. Even now, his joy lifts me. Even now, his memory gives me strength. This journey has taken me through depths I never expected, but it has also shown me the power of love that refuses to die.

This is not the ending of our story. It is the beginning of the part where healing grows from pain. Where purpose rises from loss. Where hope returns slowly but surely. And where love shows itself stronger than any darkness.

This book exists because he lived.

And because he lived, his story will continue to touch hearts long after mine stops beating.

Wherever he is now, I imagine him turning toward the sky, laughing, and dancing with a freedom only heaven can hold. And I whisper into the quiet moments of my life that I will see him again.

Maybe sooner than I think.

Maybe in a distant eternity.

Maybe in a moment when heaven opens just enough for love to shine through.

Until then, he dances in the sky.

And I carry him here, where love never ends.

-with love mommy

ACTIVITIES

A Peaceful Image

It can bring great comfort to imagine our loved ones in a place of peace, joy, and light. When you close your eyes and think of them now, what do you see?

A Thought for Your Journal: You might like to write about the happy things you imagine them doing today. You can start with the idea: "I imagine them happy, doing..."

A Creative Vision: On a separate piece of paper, you can create a picture of your loved one in the sky. You might draw them within a soft cloud, a bright sun, or as a small figure among the stars. Draw anything that makes your heart feel peaceful when you think of them.

LETTER TO HEAVEN

Dear Bo,

I miss you every day. Your laughter, your hugs, the way you looked at the world with wonder still echo in my heart. I imagine you free now, happy, running with all your animals and smiling the way you used to when you looked up at airplanes. I hope you can hear me when I talk to you. I hope you feel my love reaching across the distance. Until we meet again, keep dancing, my sweet boy. I love you forever.

Your strength held our family together even when illness tried to tear it apart. I hope you know how much your love shaped my life. I can picture Bo, watching over me from a place where pain no longer exists. I carry your lessons. I carry your memory. I carry your love. One day, I will be with you all again.

-Mom

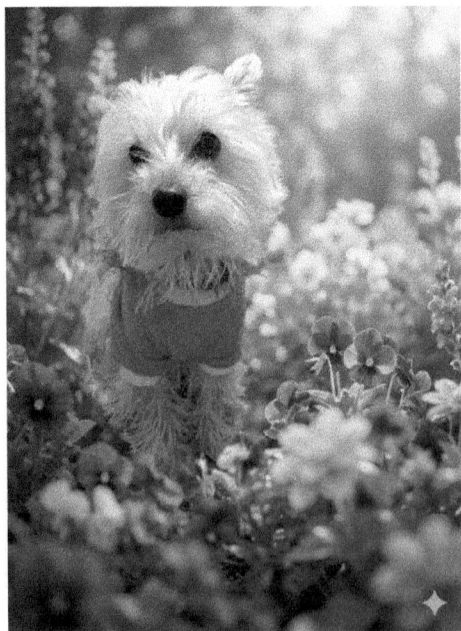

ACTIVITIES TO DO WITH YOUR FAMILY OR FRIENDS :

Continuing Your Journey of Love

The journey of remembering doesn't have to end with this book. Here are a few ways to keep your memories close:

1- **Special Activities**: You might choose to plant a flower, light a candle on special days, or visit a place that your loved one enjoyed.

2- **Honoring Every Connection**: If you are remembering more than one loved one—including special pets—you can use the prompts in this book as a guide for each of them. You may want to dedicate a separate notebook or journal to each person or animal so you have a special place for all your memories.

3- **Create a Memory Box**: Find a box or a folder to keep your "keepsakes." This is a wonderful place to store photos, drawings you've made, or small items that remind you of the love you shared.

A Special Ornament of Love

You can create a beautiful ornament to keep your loved one's memory visible in your home. This is a wonderful way to honor them during holidays or all year round.

How to create your ornament:

1. **Find a special image**: On a separate piece of paper, you can draw a beautiful frame, a heart, or a star.
2. **Add a photo**: Place a small picture of your loved one in the center of your drawing.
3. **Display with love**: With the help of an adult, you can cut out your creation from your separate paper.
4. **Choose a home for it**: Use a piece of ribbon or string to hang your ornament on a tree, display it on your door, or keep it in a special place in your room..

HOW TO MAKE A FAMILY TREE

A Gallery of Memories Think of the people and pets you love and keep their photos in a special album or frame. Looking at their pictures is a beautiful way to remember the happy times you shared together..

ACTIVITIES FOR THE LOSS OF A LOVED ONE:

Make a Palylist of movies that can help with the loss:

1. ALL DOGS GO TO HEAVEN
2. LION King
3. Moana
4. Tarzan
5. Cars 3
6. The haunted Mansion
7. Cinderella
8. Pochahontas
9. The prince and the Frog
10. Frozen 2
11. Coco
12. Bridge to Tarabithia
13. Lilo and Stitch
14. The Good Dinasour
15. Pirates of the Carribean
16. Encanto
17. The Increedibles
18. Onward
19. Mulan
20. Brother Bear
21. Finding Nemo
22. Big Hero
23. Inside out
24. Beauty and the Beast
25. Bambi
26. uP
27. Brave
28. Batman-Death in the family

29. Harry Potter
30. Spiderman
31. Superman

This is just a few but there is more.

Song That Can Help:

1. DANCING IN THE SKY- DANI AND LIZZY NELSON
2. THANKSGIVING ISNT THANKSGIVING WITHOUT YOU-TRIOLOGY SOUL
3. CHRISTMAS IN HEAVEN-PAUL MARINO AND JEREMY JOHNSON
4. I"LL FLY AWAY-JOEY AND RORY FEEK
5. Tears in Heaven-Eric Clapton
6. Halleujah-Jeff buckley
7. The Dance-Garth Brooks
8. I will remember you-Sarah McLachlan
9. See you again-Wiz Khalifaft. Charlie Puth
10. Wake me up when September ends-Green Day
11. Marjorie-Taylor Swift
12. Slipped away-Arvil Lavigne
13. In loving memory-Alter Bridge
14. Jealous of the Angels-Jean Bostic
15. Fix you- coldplay
16. Angel-Sarah McLachlan
17. One Sweet Day-Mariah Carey, Boyzz 11 Men
18. Everybody hurts-R.E.M
19. How do I say Goodbye-Dean Lewis
20. Heavens not to far-We three
21. This is what loosing someone feels like-JVKE
22. Goodbye Lover-James Blunt
23. Landslide-Fleetwood Mac
24. Wish you were hear-Lukas Graham
25. I'll be missing you-Puff Daddy, Faith Evans and 112
26. Do they have internet in Heaven-Simon Robert French
27. There are lots more of your choice

1. Make a door hanger
2. Plaster of Paris Print of your hand of foot
3. Place mats with a picture of the loved one or pet
4. Color your own book marks
5. Write down things you did with your loved ones.Even things you planned on dong with them. Even if it's animal.
6. Write down your feelings of how you feel about them going away.
7. Favorite things about the person.
8. For older kids\adults-what do you have in common {like your laugh etc..}
9. Go plant Flowers or a tree- Memory Garden.
10. Ask lots of questions-Talk
11. Go do something fun that THEY loved to do.
12. Play a favorite song or dvd or read.
13. Take a walk
14. Make a memory Book
15. Make a ornament for a tree
16. Dance
17. Bean bag toss
18. Puppet show
19. Make their favorite dessert
20. If youre feeling overwhelmed take breaths in and slowing let it out.
21. Make a keychain\bracelet with there favorite colors or name.
22. Art of favorite things
23. Paint rocks
24. Pillow fight
25. Musical chairs
26. Do something special on Hoidays\Birthdays
27. Tell stories about that person
28. Carry something of theirs with yu
29. Blow Bubbles
30. Playdoh to sculpt something
31. Take s teashirt\shirt put it on a teddybear
32. Paint a picture

33. Put a puzzle together
34. Take the persons name like PAPA and look for things around the house with those letters
35. Color the tree of life and add names
36. Cut out Angels and put their picture in the head part
37. Get a piece of foam board and glue pictures on it.

1. They place thoughts in our head. Because they In spirit form, our loved ones don't have an audible voice. Therefore, they give us messages telepathically. Pay attention to thoughts that just "pop" into your head.

2. They love to play with electricity on and off, flicker lights, turn the television and radio on and off. An they make appliances beep for no apparent reason.

3. They make buzzing noises in our ears, Because our loved ones speak to us on a different, higher frequency, we may hear ringing in our ears when they are trying to get our attention.

4. . They allow us to feel peaceful for no reason. When our loved ones are in the room, they usually make us feel so loved and at peace. It usually happens at the most unsuspecting time, so there is no logical explanation for our sudden bliss.

5. They place common objects such as feathers, coins, or rocks in our path. Our loved ones like to place things over and over again in our path that were significant to them.

6. They give off fragrances. ° We can often tell our deceased loved ones are around us when we smell their perfume, flowers, cigar or cigarrete smoke, or any other familiar smell they had.

7. You so thought they were sitting at the table or standing behind you, you had to double-take

8. You keep forgetting that they aren't 'there

9. You are inspired to make their favorite dish, drink, or play their favorite music

10. Wtch how your animal is reacting. You pet might have an
    encounter with 'thin air' .. meaning your loved one

THE FOUR TAKS OF GRIEF
THAT ACTUALLY MAKE SENSE

Here's task 1.

Accept the reality of the loss. Not mentally. Your brain can know they're gone long before your body accepts it.

This takes time. Task 2.

Feel the pain of your grief. Your isn't to be strong. It is to build the capacity to feel what hurts without abonding yourself.

And then task 3.

Adjus to a world without the person that you love physically, emotionally, spiritually. Your identity changes. Your life structure changes.

Everything changes. And then task 4.

Find an enduring connection with them while building a life around the loss. This one saved me. It gave me persmission to stay connected to loved ones. To talk to them, honour them. Carry them while still moving.

The Arc of New Mexico 5130 Masthead St. NE Albuquerque, NM 87109

Contact Us
Phone: (505) 883-4630
Toll Free: (800) 358-6493
Fax: (505) 883-5564

Guardianship & Care Management Services LLC
1201 Eubank Blvd NE Ste 7
Albuquerque, NM 87112
(505) 480-6541

If you can't say what's in your heart, say it your way. oo Even if your voice is rusty. Even if all you can manage is a wagging tail.

Help with trying to change laws on Guardianship and Health Care For the Disabled/Handicap

1. Mail to. Centralized Case Management Operations. U.S. Department of Health and Human Services. 200 Independence Avenue, SW. Room 509F HHH Bldg. Washington, D.C. 20201.

2. Email to OCRComplaint@hhs.gov.
https://www.hhs.gov
Complaint Process - HHS.gov

Contact the New Mexico Courts Guardianship Program or the NM Office of Guardianship for referrals to professional guardians or case managers.

Search for "Guardianship Specialists" or "Guardianship Counselors" in your area via organizations like The Arc or private firms.

New Mexico Developmental Disabilities Council
nmddc.org

THE LAST DEPARTURE TO HEAVEN !!!